GALVESTON DIET COOKBOOK FOR BEGINNERS:

Quick and delicious Hormone-Balancing Recipes to Reduce Inflammation and Aid Weight Loss

BY

DIANA FRANQUI

First published by Diana Franqui Copyright © 2023 by Diana Franqui

mechanical, photocopying, recording, scanning, or otherwise, without written permission from the publisher. It is illegal to copy this book, post it to a website, or distribute it by any other means without permission

<u>TABLE OF CONTENTS</u>

INTRODUCTION

In a world inundated with an overwhelming array of diet

fads and nutrition trends, it can be challenging to find a

sustainable and scientifically sound approach to eating well and achieving lasting health. The Galveston Diet Cookbook for Beginners, a culinary treasure trove designed to transform your relationship with food, stands as a beacon of hope and practicality amidst this nutritional chaos. This cookbook, a natural extension of the groundbreaking Galveston Diet, not only simplifies the art of eating healthily but also offers a delectable path towards improved vitality and well-being.

Nestled in the heart of Texas, Galveston Island is not just a picturesque coastal destination; it's
also the birthplace of a unique dietary approach that has garnered recognition for its holistic and scientifically-backed principles. Developed by renowned physician Dr. Mary Claire Haver, the Galveston Diet is rooted in the wisdom of women's bodies and the significant impact of hormonal changes on overall health and wellness. With a deep understanding of the body's natural rhythms, Dr. Haver has crafted a diet plan that resonates with women of all ages and stages of life,

providing not just a means for weight management but a pathway to genuine nourishment and hormonal balance.

As the sun-kissed shores of Galveston Island beckon, the Galveston Diet Cookbook for Beginners beckons you into the heart of a healthful and flavor-rich journey. Within its pages, you'll find a cornucopia of sumptuous recipes, meticulously curated and designed to empower you to make informed, delicious, and health-conscious food choices. Whether you're new to the Galveston Diet or simply seeking to enrich your culinary repertoire with recipes that prioritize your well-being, this cookbook is your ideal companion.

It's not just another cookbook; it's a holistic approach to nutrition and well-being. The Galveston Diet Cookbook for Beginners embraces the fundamental principle that food is medicine, and every meal can be a source of nourishment and healing. Through the gentle guidance of this cookbook, you will embark on a transformative journey that harmonizes the art of cooking with the science of nutrition. Here, you'll discover the essential concepts that underpin the Galveston Diet, from the role of

hormones in women's health to the significance of balanced macronutrients.

This cookbook doesn't just stop at providing an extensive collection of delectable recipes; it empowers you with the knowledge to understand why these recipes are not only delicious but also crucial for your well-being. It's a true testament to the adage that knowledge is power. By the time you've explored the pages of this cookbook, you'll not only be a skilled home chef but also a well-informed advocate for your own health.

Join us on this culinary adventure, where the vibrant flavors of fresh, whole foods intermingle with the science-backed wisdom of the Galveston Diet. Prepare to unlock the secrets of hormonal balance, bolster your energy levels, and create a stronger foundation for lifelong

health. The Galveston Diet Cookbook for Beginners is more than just a cookbook; it's your passport to a revitalized you, one delicious and nutritious recipe at a time. So, don your apron, sharpen your knives, and get ready to embark on a transformative culinary journey towards health and vitality. Your kitchen will become the laboratory where you cook up a healthier, happier, and more balanced life.

CHAPTER 1: THE GALVESTON DIET: A HORMONE BALANCING APPROACH TO HEALTH

How Hormones Affect Weight and Inflammation

In the quest for optimal health and well-being, understanding the intricate relationship between hormones, weight management, and inflammation is crucial. Hormones play a significant role in our bodies, influencing everything from metabolism to mood. The Galveston Diet is an emerging approach that focuses on hormone balancing to promote

sustainable weight loss and reduce inflammation. This innovative dietary plan is gaining recognition for its ability to empower individuals to take control of their health. Let's delve into the science of how hormones affect weight and inflammation and explore the principles of the Galveston Diet.

The Hormone-Weight-Inflammation Connection

Hormones are chemical messengers produced by various glands in the endocrine system. They regulate vital bodily functions, including metabolism, appetite, and inflammation. When these hormones become imbalanced, they can lead to weight gain and increased inflammation.

Insulin: One of the most well-known hormones, insulin, regulates blood sugar levels. An overproduction of insulin, often caused by a diet high in refined carbohydrates, can lead to insulin resistance and weight gain.

Leptin: Leptin is responsible for signaling feelings of fullness. When your body becomes resistant to leptin, it can lead to overeating and weight gain.

Cortisol: Known as the stress hormone, cortisol can be elevated due to chronic stress. High cortisol levels can contribute to fat storage, particularly around the abdomen.

Estrogen: An imbalance in estrogen levels, particularly during menopause, can lead to weight gain and increased inflammation.

Inflammation: Chronic inflammation is linked to numerous health problems, including obesity. It can disrupt hormonal balance and contribute to insulin resistance.

The Galveston Diet Approach

Developed by Dr. Mary Claire Haver, a board-certified OB-GYN, the Galveston Diet is designed to address hormone imbalances that often plague women during perimenopause and menopause. The primary goal of the Galveston Diet is to restore hormonal balance, leading to improved weight management and reduced inflammation. Here are some key principles of the Galveston Diet:

Balanced Macronutrients: The diet emphasizes a balanced intake of macronutrients, including healthy fats, lean proteins, and complex

carbohydrates, to support stable blood sugar levels and hormone regulation.

Intermittent Fasting: Dr. Haver recommends intermittent fasting to help the body become more insulin sensitive, which can aid in weight loss and hormone balance.

Inflammation-Reducing Foods: The diet encourages the consumption of anti-inflammatory foods, such as fatty fish, leafy greens, and colorful vegetables, to combat chronic inflammation.

Stress Reduction: Managing stress is vital for hormonal balance. The Galveston Diet promotes stress-reduction techniques like yoga, meditation, and mindfulness.

Supplements: Some women may benefit from supplements like omega-3 fatty acids, vitamin D, and magnesium to support hormone balance.

Benefits of the Galveston Diet

By addressing hormone imbalances, the Galveston Diet offers numerous potential benefits:

Weight Management: Restoring hormonal balance can help women lose weight and maintain a healthy weight more easily.

Reduced Inflammation: By promoting an anti-inflammatory diet, the Galveston Diet can alleviate symptoms associated with inflammation-related conditions.

Increased Energy: Stable blood sugar levels and improved hormone regulation can result in increased energy and vitality.

Improved Mood: Hormone balance can positively impact mood and emotional well-being.

The Galveston Diet is an innovative approach to health that recognizes the critical role hormones play in weight management and inflammation. By addressing hormone imbalances through dietary changes, stress reduction, and targeted supplements, this diet offers a path to better health and well-being, particularly for women navigating the challenges of perimenopause and menopause. It's essential to consult with a healthcare professional before making any significant dietary changes, but the Galveston

Diet represents a promising strategy for those seeking a hormone-balancing approach to health.

Getting Started with the Galveston Diet

In a world where diet trends come and go, the Galveston Diet stands out as a unique and effective approach to achieving better health through hormone balance. Created by Dr. Mary Claire Haver, a board-certified obstetrician and gynecologist, this innovative diet plan specifically addresses the needs of women over 40, whose hormonal changes can make weight loss and overall well-being more challenging. The Galveston Diet focuses on harnessing the power of hormones to help women achieve their health and fitness goals, and it has gained significant attention for its remarkable results.

Understanding the Galveston Diet Philosophy Before diving into the details of the Galveston Diet, it's essential to understand the core philosophy behind this approach. Dr. Haver's program is rooted in the idea that hormonal imbalances can wreak havoc on a woman's metabolism, energy levels, and overall health. As women age, hormonal fluctuations, particularly in estrogen and insulin, can lead to weight gain, sleep disturbances, mood swings, and more. The Galveston Diet recognizes the significance of these hormonal changes and aims to restore balance to help women feel their best.

The Four Pillars of the Galveston Diet

The Galveston Diet is built on four fundamental pillars:

Nutrient Timing

The diet encourages women to be mindful of when they eat, with a focus on balancing blood sugar levels and supporting hormone regulation. By eating during specific windows and being conscious of nutrient timing, women can enhance their metabolism and promote better hormonal balance.

Whole Foods

Emphasizing the consumption of whole, nutrient-dense foods, the Galveston Diet encourages a diet rich in vegetables, lean proteins, healthy fats, and complex carbohydrates. These choices support hormonal health and overall well-being.

Fasting

Intermittent fasting plays a pivotal role in the Galveston Diet. Fasting periods, carefully timed with meals, help improve insulin sensitivity and support hormonal balance, contributing to more effective weight management.

Stress Reduction

Stress can have a profound impact on hormonal health. The Galveston Diet promotes stress-reduction techniques like mindfulness, meditation, and adequate sleep to optimize hormone balance and well-being.

Getting Started

Starting the Galveston Diet is a straightforward process, but it's essential to be committed and dedicated to your health journey. Here are some steps to help you get started:

Educate Yourself

Before diving in, take the time to learn about the Galveston Diet. Read Dr. Mary Claire Haver's book "The Galveston Diet" or explore the resources available on the official website. Understanding the principles behind the diet will help you stay motivated and informed.

Assess Your Goals

Define your specific health and wellness goals. Whether you want to lose weight, improve your energy levels, or manage hormone-related issues, having clear objectives will guide your journey.

Plan Your Meals

The Galveston Diet is built on balanced, whole foods. Create a meal plan that aligns with the

principles of the diet, including nutrient timing, fasting, and stress reduction techniques.

Start Slowly

Transitioning into the Galveston Diet can be easier if you start gradually. You don't need to make all the changes at once. Consider incorporating intermittent fasting into your routine or swapping out processed foods for whole, nutrient-dense options one step at a time.

Track Your Progress

Keep a journal to monitor your food intake, exercise, and how you're feeling. This will help you stay on track and make necessary adjustments to meet your goals.

Seek Support

Consider joining the Galveston Diet community, either through the official online forums or social media groups. Connecting with others who are on a similar journey can provide valuable support and motivation.

The Galveston Diet is not a one-size-fits-all solution, and it may require some adjustments to suit your individual needs and preferences. However, by focusing on the four pillars of nutrient timing, whole foods, fasting, and stress reduction, you can embark on a journey to better hormonal balance, improved health, and increased vitality. Remember that any significant dietary changes should be discussed with a healthcare professional, especially if you have pre-existing medical conditions or concerns.

If you're a woman over 40 looking for a sustainable, science-based approach to improve your health and well-being, the Galveston Diet offers a promising path toward a balanced and healthier future.

Tips for Success on Your Galveston Diet Journey

The Galveston Diet is not just another fad diet; it's a science-backed approach to weight loss and overall health. Created by Dr. Mary Claire Haver, a board-certified OB-GYN, this diet is designed to address hormone imbalances that can lead to weight gain and other health issues. By focusing on hormone-balancing foods, intermittent fasting, and lifestyle changes, the Galveston Diet offers a comprehensive and sustainable path to better health. To ensure your success on this journey, here are some key tips to keep in mind.

Understand the Hormone Connection:

The Galveston Diet is rooted in the understanding that hormonal changes,

particularly those experienced during menopause, can disrupt your body's natural balance and lead to weight gain. By addressing these hormonal fluctuations, you can boost your metabolism and regain control over your health.

Embrace Hormone-Balancing Foods:

The foundation of the Galveston Diet is hormone-balancing foods. This includes plenty of fruits and vegetables, lean proteins, healthy fats, and whole grains. These foods not only help balance hormones but also provide essential nutrients for overall well-being.

Practice Intermittent Fasting:

Intermittent fasting is a key component of the Galveston Diet. By incorporating periods of fasting into your eating schedule, you allow your body to tap into its fat stores for energy. This can

lead to weight loss and improved insulin sensitivity.

Start Slowly:

If you're new to intermittent fasting, don't jump in too quickly. Dr. Haver recommends starting with a 12-hour fasting window and gradually increasing it to 14-16 hours as your body adjusts. This gradual approach can help minimize discomfort and improve long-term adherence.

Stay Hydrated:

Proper hydration is crucial for hormone balance and overall health. Make sure to drink plenty of water throughout the day to support your body's natural processes.

Prioritize Quality Sleep:

Getting enough quality sleep is essential for hormone regulation. Aim for 7-8 hours of restful sleep each night to support your weight loss and overall well-being.

Monitor Your Progress:

Keep track of your meals, fasting times, and how you feel each day. This can help you identify patterns and adjust your approach if needed.

Seek Support:

Embarking on a new dietary and lifestyle journey can be challenging, so consider finding a support system. Whether it's a friend, family member, or online community, having others to share your experiences with can make the process more enjoyable.

Be Patient:

Hormone balancing and weight loss take time. It's essential to be patient with your body as it adjusts to the new dietary and lifestyle changes. Remember that progress may not always be linear.

Consult a Healthcare Professional:

Before making any significant changes to your diet or lifestyle, it's advisable to consult a healthcare professional. They can help you assess your specific needs and ensure that the Galveston Diet is a suitable choice for you.

The Galveston Diet is a hormone-balancing approach to health that offers a sustainable path to weight loss and overall well-being. By embracing hormone-balancing foods, intermittent fasting, and making thoughtful

lifestyle changes, you can regain control over your health and vitality. Remember, success on this journey is a process, and with the right mindset and support, you can achieve your health and wellness goals.

CHAPTER 2: BREAKFAST RECIPES ENERGIZING MORNING START

Avocado and Spinach Omelette

Time Frame: 15-20 minutes

Ingredients:

- *2 eggs*
- *1/4 cup chopped spinach*
- *1/4 avocado, sliced*
- *Salt and pepper to taste*
- *1 tablespoon olive oil*
- *Optional: shredded cheese or diced tomatoes*

Instructions:

- *Heat the olive oil in a non-stick skillet over medium heat.*
- *Whisk the eggs in a bowl and season with salt and pepper.*
- *Pour the whisked eggs into the skillet.*
- *As the eggs begin to set, add the spinach and avocado slices.*

- *Cook until the omelette is set and slightly browned on the bottom, then fold it in half.*

- *Optionally, sprinkle some shredded cheese or diced tomatoes on top.*

- *Slide the omelette onto a plate and serve hot.*

Tip:

- *Be careful not to overcook the omelette. It should be slightly runny on top when you fold it, as residual heat will continue to cook it.*

Blueberry Chia Seed Pudding

Time Frame: 10 minutes (plus chilling time)

Ingredients:

- *1/4 cup chia seeds*
- *1 cup almond milk or your preferred milk*
- *1/2 teaspoon vanilla extract*
- *1 tablespoon honey or maple syrup*
- *1/2 cup fresh blueberries*

Instructions:

- *In a bowl, mix the chia seeds, almond milk, vanilla extract, and honey or maple syrup.*

- *Stir well, ensuring there are no clumps of chia seeds.*

- *Refrigerate for at least 2-3 hours or overnight, allowing it to thicken.*

- *Top with fresh blueberries before serving.*

Tip:

- *You can make this the night before for a quick and healthy breakfast in the morning.*

Greek Yogurt Parfait with Berries

Time Frame: 5 minutes

Ingredients:

- *1 cup Greek yogurt*
- *1/2 cup mixed berries (strawberries, blueberries, raspberries)*
- *2 tablespoons honey*
- *1/4 cup granola*

Instructions:

- *Start with a layer of Greek yogurt in a glass or bowl.*

- *Add a layer of mixed berries.*
- *Drizzle honey on top.*
- *Sprinkle granola over the berries.*

- *Repeat the layers if desired.*
- *Serve immediately.*

Breakfast Quinoa Bowl

Time Frame: 20-25 minutes

Ingredients:

- *1/2 cup quinoa*
- *1 cup water or milk*
- *1/2 teaspoon cinnamon*
- *1/4 cup sliced almonds*
- *1/4 cup dried fruits (e.g., raisins, apricots)*
- *1 tablespoon honey*
- *Sliced bananas or berries (optional)*

Instructions:

- *Rinse the quinoa thoroughly.*
- *In a saucepan, combine quinoa, water or milk, and cinnamon. Bring to a boil.*
- *Reduce heat, cover, and simmer for 15-20 minutes, or until quinoa is cooked and liquid is absorbed.*
- *Fluff the quinoa with a fork.*
- *Serve in a bowl, top with sliced almonds, dried fruits, honey, and sliced bananas or berries if desired.*

Tip:

- *You can make a large batch of quinoa and store it in the fridge for quick breakfasts throughout the week.*

Green Smoothie Delight

Time Frame: 5 minutes

Ingredients:

- *1 cup spinach or kale*
- *1/2 banana*
- *1/2 cup Greek yogurt*
- *1/2 cup almond milk or water*
- *1 tablespoon honey or maple syrup*
- *1/2 cup frozen mango or pineapple chunks*
- *Ice cubes (optional)*

Instructions:

- *Place all the ingredients in a blender.*
- *Blend until smooth.*
- *Add more liquid if needed for your preferred consistency.*
- *Serve immediately.*

Sweet Potato Hash and Eggs

Time Frame: 25-30 minutes

Ingredients:

- *2 medium sweet potatoes, peeled and diced*
- *1 onion, chopped*
- *2 tablespoons olive oil*
- *1/2 teaspoon paprika*
- *Salt and pepper to taste*
- *4 eggs*

Instructions:

- *Heat the olive oil in a skillet over medium heat.*
- *Add the diced sweet potatoes and chopped onion.*
- *Season with paprika, salt, and pepper.*
- *Cook, stirring occasionally, until the sweet potatoes are tender and slightly crispy (about 15-20 minutes).*
- *Create four wells in the hash and crack an egg into each well.*
- *Cover the skillet and cook for about 5-7 minutes, or until the eggs are cooked to your desired level.*
- *Serve hot.*

Tip:

You can customize the seasonings in the sweet potato hash to your preference by adding herbs or spices like rosemary, thyme, or cayenne pepper.

CHAPTER 3: LUNCH RECIPES MIDDAY NUTRIENT BOOST

Avocado and Spinach Omelette

Time Frame: 15-20 minutes

Ingredients:

- *2 large eggs*
- *1/2 ripe avocado, sliced*
- *Handful of fresh spinach leaves*
- *Salt and pepper to taste*
- *Olive oil for cooking (optional)*
- *Grated cheese (optional)*

Instructions:

- *Heat a non-stick skillet over medium-high heat.*

- *If using olive oil, add a small amount to the skillet.*

- *In a bowl, whisk the eggs and season with salt and pepper.*

- *Pour the whisked eggs into the skillet and swirl them around to create an even layer.*

- *Add the avocado slices and spinach on one side of the omelette.*

- *If desired, sprinkle grated cheese over the toppings.*

- *Once the edges of the omelette start to set, carefully fold the other half over the toppings.*

- *Cook for another minute or until the omelette is set but still slightly runny in the center.*

- *Fold the omelette in half and slide it onto a plate.*

Tip:

Be gentle when flipping the omelette to prevent it from breaking.

Blueberry Chia Seed Pudding

Time Frame: 5 minutes (plus chilling time)

Ingredients:

- *1/4 cup chia seeds*
- *1 cup milk (almond, coconut, or any of your choice)*
- *1 tablespoon honey or maple syrup*
- *1/2 teaspoon vanilla extract*
- *1/2 cup fresh blueberries*

Instructions:

- *In a bowl, combine chia seeds, milk, honey, and vanilla extract.*
- *Stir well, ensuring that the chia seeds are evenly distributed.*
- *Let the mixture sit for a few minutes, then stir again to prevent clumping.*
- *Cover the bowl and refrigerate for at least 2 hours or overnight.*
- *Before serving, top with fresh blueberries.*

Tip:

You can add more sweetener or toppings like nuts and coconut flakes for extra flavor and texture.

Greek Yogurt Parfait with Berries

Time Frame: 5 minutes

Ingredients:

- *1 cup Greek yogurt*
- *1/2 cup granola*
- *1/2 cup mixed berries (strawberries, blueberries, raspberries)*

- *Honey or maple syrup (optional)*

Instructions:

- *In a glass or bowl, start with a layer of Greek yogurt.*

- *Add a layer of granola.*

- *Top with a layer of mixed berries.*
- *Repeat the layers until you've used all the ingredients.*

- *Drizzle honey or maple syrup on top for sweetness (if desired).*

Tip:

- *Customize this parfait with your favorite fruits and nuts for added variety.*

Breakfast Quinoa Bowl

Time Frame: 20-25 minutes

Ingredients:

- *1/2 cup quinoa*
- *1 cup milk (almond, soy, etc.)*
- *1 tablespoon honey or maple syrup*
- *1/2 teaspoon cinnamon*
- *Sliced bananas*
- *Chopped nuts (e.g., almonds, walnuts)*

- *Dried fruits (e.g., raisins, apricots)*

Instructions:

- *Rinse the quinoa and cook it in milk according to package instructions.*
- *Stir in honey or maple syrup and cinnamon.*
- *Serve in a bowl topped with sliced bananas, chopped nuts, and dried fruits.*

Tip:

- *Experiment with different fruits and nuts to suit your taste.*

Green Smoothie Delight

Time Frame: 5 minutes

Ingredients:

- *2 cups fresh spinach leaves*
- *1 ripe banana*
- *1/2 cup pineapple chunks*
- *1/2 cup almond milk*
- *1 tablespoon honey (optional)*
- *Ice cubes (optional)*

Instructions:

- *Combine all the ingredients in a blender.*

- *Blend until smooth.*
- *Add ice cubes if you want a colder smoothie.*

- *Tip: Feel free to adjust the sweetness with honey or add protein powder for an extra boost.*

Sweet Potato Hash and Eggs

Time Frame: 25-30 minutes

Ingredients:

- *2 medium sweet potatoes, peeled and diced*
- *1 small onion, chopped*
- *2 cloves garlic, minced*
- *2 tablespoons olive oil*
- *4 eggs*
- *Salt and pepper to taste*
- *Fresh herbs for garnish (e.g., parsley)*

Instructions:

- *Heat olive oil in a skillet over medium heat.*

- *Add the sweet potatoes and onions and cook until they're softened and slightly crispy, stirring occasionally.*

- *Add the minced garlic and continue to cook for another minute.*

- *Make four wells in the hash and crack an egg into each well.*
- *Cover the skillet and cook until the eggs are done to your liking.*
- *Season with salt and pepper and garnish with fresh herbs.*

Tip:

- *You can add other vegetables like bell peppers or spinach to the hash for extra flavor and nutrition.*

Enjoy your delicious and nutritious breakfast options!

CHAPTER 4: DINNER RECIPES SATISFYING EVENING MEALS

Baked Salmon with Lemon-Dill Sauce

Time Frame: Approximately 30-35 minutes.

Ingredients:

- *4 salmon fillets*
- *Salt and pepper to taste*
- *2 tablespoons olive oil*

- *1/4 cup fresh lemon juice*
- *2 tablespoons chopped fresh dill*
- *1 clove garlic, minced*

Instructions:

- *Preheat your oven to 375°F (190°C).*
- *Season the salmon fillets with salt and pepper.*
- *In an ovenproof dish, drizzle olive oil, place the salmon fillets, and bake for about 15-20 minutes, or until the salmon flakes easily.*
- *While the salmon is baking, prepare the sauce by mixing lemon juice, dill, and minced garlic.*
- *Once the salmon is done, drizzle the lemon-dill sauce over it before serving.*

Tips:

- *Be careful not to overcook the salmon, as it can become dry. Use a fork to check for doneness; it should easily flake.*

Zucchini Noodles with Pesto and Cherry Tomatoes

Time Frame: Approximately 15-20 minutes.

Ingredients:

- *3-4 zucchinis, spiralized into noodles*
- *1 cup cherry tomatoes, halved*
- *1/2 cup pesto sauce (homemade or store-bought)*
- *Parmesan cheese for garnish (optional)*

Instructions:

- *Spiralize the zucchinis into noodles using a spiralizer.*

- *In a pan, sauté the cherry tomatoes in a little olive oil for 3-4 minutes until they soften.*

- *Add the zucchini noodles and pesto sauce, tossing everything together for about 2-3 minutes until the zucchini noodles are tender.*

- *Serve hot, and garnish with Parmesan cheese if desired.*

Tips:

- *Zucchini noodles can get watery, so be sure not to overcook them. You can also pat them dry with a paper towel before adding the sauce.*

Turkey and Sweet Potato Casserole

Time Frame: Approximately 1 hour.

Ingredients:

- *1 pound ground turkey*
- *2 large sweet potatoes, peeled and sliced*
- *1 onion, chopped*
- *2 cloves garlic, minced*
- *1 cup shredded cheddar cheese*
- *1 cup chicken or turkey broth*
- *1 teaspoon dried thyme*
- *Salt and pepper to taste*

Instructions:

- *Preheat your oven to 375°F (190°C).*

- *In a skillet, brown the ground turkey with onions and garlic. Season with thyme, salt, and pepper.*

- *In a greased casserole dish, layer sweet potato slices, turkey mixture, and cheese.*

- *Repeat the layers until you run out of ingredients, finishing with a layer of cheese on top.*

- *Pour the broth over the casserole.*

- *Cover with foil and bake for 45 minutes. Uncover and bake for an additional 15 minutes until the sweet potatoes are tender and the top is golden.*

Tips:

- *You can add some fresh herbs or breadcrumbs for extra flavor and texture on the top layer.*

Vegetarian Chili

Time Frame: Approximately 30-40 minutes.

Ingredients:

- *2 cans of kidney beans, drained and rinsed*
- *1 can of black beans, drained and rinsed*
- *1 can of diced tomatoes*
- *1 onion, chopped*
- *1 bell pepper, chopped*
- *2 cloves garlic, minced*
- *2 tablespoons chili powder*
- *1 teaspoon cumin*
- *Salt and pepper to taste*
- *Optional toppings: shredded cheese, sour cream, chopped cilantro, chopped scallions*

Instructions:

- *In a large pot, sauté the onions, garlic, and bell pepper until softened.*
- *Add the chili powder and cumin, stirring for a minute.*
- *Add the beans and diced tomatoes. Season with salt and pepper.*
- *Simmer for 20-30 minutes until the chili thickens.*
- *Serve with your choice of toppings.*

Tips:

- *You can adjust the level of spiciness by adding more or less chili powder. You can also add corn, carrots, or other vegetables for extra flavor and nutrition.*

Balsamic Glazed Chicken with Roasted Vegetables

Time Frame: Approximately 40-45 minutes.

Ingredients:

- *4 boneless, skinless chicken breasts*
- *1 pound mixed vegetables (e.g., broccoli, bell peppers, carrots)*

- *1/4 cup balsamic vinegar*
- *2 tablespoons olive oil*
- *2 cloves garlic, minced*
- *1 teaspoon dried oregano*
- *Salt and pepper to taste*

Instructions:

- *Preheat your oven to 400°F (200°C).*
- *In a bowl, whisk together balsamic vinegar, olive oil, minced garlic, oregano, salt, and pepper.*
- *Place the chicken breasts and vegetables on a baking sheet. Drizzle the balsamic mixture over them.*
- *Roast in the oven for 25-30 minutes or until the chicken is cooked through, and the vegetables are tender.*

Tips:

- *You can marinate the chicken in the balsamic mixture for extra flavor, or use your favorite vegetables for roasting.*

Spaghetti Squash with Mushroom Alfredo Sauce

Time Frame: Approximately 45-50 minutes.

Ingredients:

- *1 spaghetti squash*
- *2 cups sliced mushrooms*
- *1 cup heavy cream*
- *1/2 cup grated Parmesan cheese*
- *2 cloves garlic, minced*
- *2 tablespoons butter*
- *Salt and pepper to taste*
- *Fresh parsley for garnish*

Instructions:

- *Preheat your oven to 375°F (190°C).*

- *Cut the spaghetti squash in half, scoop out the seeds, and roast it in the oven for 30-40 minutes until tender.*

- *While the squash is roasting, sauté the mushrooms in butter until they release their liquid and become tender. Add minced garlic and cook for a minute.*

- *Pour in the heavy cream and grated Parmesan, stirring until the sauce thickens. Season with salt and pepper.*

- *Use a fork to scrape the cooked spaghetti squash into strands.*

- *Serve the mushroom Alfredo sauce over the spaghetti squash and garnish with fresh parsley.*

Tips:

- *Make sure not to overcook the squash; it should still have some firmness to it. You can use a variety of mushrooms for extra flavor. If the sauce is too thick, you can add a bit of pasta cooking water to reach your desired consistency.*

Enjoy cooking these delicious recipes!

CHAPTER 5: SNACK RECIPES NOURISHING MINI-MEALS

Hummus and Veggie Sticks

Time Frame: 10-15 minutes.

Ingredients:

- *1 cup of canned chickpeas (drained and rinsed)*

- *1/4 cup of fresh lemon juice*

- *1/4 cup of tahini*
- *1 small garlic clove, minced*
- *2 tablespoons extra-virgin olive oil*

- *1/2 teaspoon ground cumin*
- *Salt and pepper to taste*
- *Assorted veggie sticks (carrots, cucumbers, bell peppers, etc.)*

Instructions:

- *Place all the ingredients (except the veggie sticks) in a food processor.*

- *Blend until smooth and creamy. You may need to scrape down the sides of the bowl as you go.*

- *Taste and adjust the seasoning as needed.*

- *Serve with your choice of veggie sticks.*

Tips:

- *If the hummus is too thick, you can add a little water to reach your desired consistency.*

- *Customize the flavor by adding additional ingredients like roasted red pepper, paprika, or pine nuts.*

Almond Butter and Banana Slices

Time Frame: 5 minutes.

Ingredients:

- *Ripe bananas*
- *Almond butter (or any nut butter)*
- *Optional: honey, chia seeds, or cinnamon*

Instructions:

- *Slice the bananas into rounds.*
- *Spread a little almond butter on each banana slice.*
- *Drizzle with honey or sprinkle with chia seeds or cinnamon if desired.*

Tips:

- *You can also use other nut butters like peanut butter or cashew butter.*
- *Feel free to add a sprinkle of your favorite seeds or spices for extra flavor and texture.*

Greek Yogurt with Honey and Walnuts

Time Frame: 5 minutes.

Ingredients:

- *Greek yogurt*
- *Honey*
- *Chopped walnuts*

Instructions:

- *Scoop Greek yogurt into a serving bowl.*
- *Drizzle honey over the yogurt.*
- *Sprinkle chopped walnuts on top.*

Tips:

- *You can add fresh berries or dried fruits for extra sweetness and texture.*

- *Consider using flavored Greek yogurt for added variety.*

Cottage Cheese with Pineapple

Time Frame: 5 minutes.

Ingredients:

- *Cottage cheese*
- *Fresh or canned pineapple chunks*

Instructions:

- *Spoon cottage cheese into a serving dish.*
- *Top with pineapple chunks.*

Tips:

- *Use fresh pineapple for the best flavor, but canned pineapple works in a pinch.*

Guacamole and Salsa with Whole-Grain Chips

Time Frame: 15-20 minutes.

Ingredients:

Guacamole:

- *3 ripe avocados*
- *1 small red onion, finely chopped*
- *1-2 tomatoes, diced*
- *2 cloves of garlic, minced*
- *Juice of 2 limes*
- *1/4 cup chopped fresh cilantro*

Salt and pepper to taste Salsa:

- *2-3 ripe tomatoes, diced*
- *1 small red onion, finely chopped*
- *1 jalapeño pepper, seeds removed and finely chopped (adjust for spiciness)*
- *Juice of 1 lime*
- *1/4 cup chopped fresh cilantro*
- *Salt and pepper to taste*

Instructions:

Guacamole:

- *Cut the avocados in half, remove the pits, and scoop the flesh into a bowl.*

- *Mash the avocados with a fork or potato masher, leaving some chunks for texture.*
- *Add the chopped red onion, diced tomatoes, minced garlic, lime juice, and cilantro to the mashed avocados.*
- *Season with salt and pepper, and mix well. Adjust lime, salt, and pepper to taste.*

Salsa:

- *In a separate bowl, combine the diced tomatoes, chopped red onion, jalapeño, lime juice, and cilantro.*
- *Season with salt and pepper, and mix well.*

Tips:

- *For a milder salsa, remove the seeds and membrane from the jalapeño.*
- *Serve with whole-grain or multigrain tortilla chips for a healthier option.*
- *If you have extra lime juice, consider squeezing some onto the guacamole to prevent browning.*
- *You can also add other ingredients to your guacamole or salsa, such as diced red bell*

peppers, corn, or black beans for added flavor and texture.

Mixed Nuts and Dried Fruits

Time Frame: Instant.

Ingredients:

- *A mixture of your favorite nuts (almonds, cashews, walnuts, etc.)*
- *An assortment of dried fruits (raisins, apricots, figs, etc.)*

Instructions:

- *Simply combine a handful of mixed nuts with a handful of dried fruits in a bowl or on a platter.*

Tips:

- *You can create your own custom mix of nuts and dried fruits based on your preferences.*
- *This is a convenient and healthy snack to have on hand for quick energy and nutrition.*
- *Enjoy these quick and easy snack recipes!*

CONCLUSION

In conclusion, the "Galveston Diet Cookbook for Beginners" has provided us with a flavorful and nourishing journey towards a healthier lifestyle. With its quick and delicious hormone-balancing recipes aimed at reducing inflammation and aiding weight loss, this book has not only given us the tools to transform our eating habits but has also empowered us with a deeper understanding of the connection between our hormones, inflammation, and overall well-being.

As we close the pages of this cookbook, we can't help but reflect on the valuable insights it has offered. From understanding the importance of balanced hormones to the impact of inflammation on our health, this book has enlightened us about the intricate relationship

between what we eat and how we feel. It has armed us with a diverse array of recipes that not only tantalize the taste buds but also support our health goals, making the journey to weight loss and well-being a delicious one.

The authors have taken us on a culinary adventure that celebrates real, whole foods and showcases how vibrant and satisfying a hormone-balancing diet can be. The simplicity and accessibility of the recipes make them suitable for all, especially beginners who may be embarking on their health and weight loss journeys for the first time. The detailed instructions, nutritional information, and tips throughout the book make it easy to navigate the recipes and adapt them to individual preferences and dietary needs.

Moreover, the "Galveston Diet Cookbook for Beginners" reinforces the notion that healthy eating is not a one-size-fits-all approach. It encourages us to be mindful of our bodies and emphasizes that each of us has unique nutritional requirements. This personalized approach to healthy eating is not only refreshing but also highly effective in achieving long-term wellness goals.

In a world where fad diets and confusing nutritional advice abound, this cookbook stands out as a reliable and practical resource. It reminds us that nourishing our bodies is a lifelong commitment, and it equips us with the tools to do so. It's a book that not only resides on our shelves but also becomes a cherished companion in our kitchens.

As we embark on our own journeys toward a healthier, happier life, we can carry the valuable lessons and mouthwatering recipes from this book with us. The "Galveston Diet Cookbook for Beginners" has opened the door to a world of possibilities where nutritious and delicious food can coexist harmoniously. It's a guide that encourages us to take charge of our health and well-being, one delectable dish at a time.

So, here's to your health, your happiness, and the many satisfying, hormone-balancing meals you'll prepare with the help of this book. May your culinary adventures be as enjoyable as they are nourishing, and may the wisdom and flavors found within these pages continue to inspire you on your lifelong journey towards a healthier you.